Swing Sisters

The Story of the International Sweethearts of Rhythm

by **KAREN DEANS** illustrated by **JOE CEPEDA**

 HOLIDAY HOUSE · NEW YORK

Library of Congress Cataloging-in-Publication Data
Deans, Karen.
Swing sisters: the story of the International Sweethearts of Rhythm / by Karen Deans;
illustrated by Joe Cepeda. — first edition. pages cm
ISBN 978-0-8234-1970-8 (hardcover)
1. International Sweethearts of Rhythm—Juvenile literature.
2. Women jazz musicians—United States—Juvenile literature.
I. Cepeda, Joe, illustrator. II. Title.
M(3930.I57D43 2015
7.8L65082-dc23
2013019683

ISBN: 978-0-8234-1970-8 (hardcover)
ISBN: 978-0-8234-5088-6 (paperback)

Way back in 1909, not far from Jackson, Mississippi, there was a special place for orphans. It was called Piney Woods Country Life School.

A man named Dr. Laurence Clifton Jones started the school. He wanted to make sure these African American kids had a place to live, food to eat, clothes to wear, and a good education. In return, the children worked at the school to earn their keep. Some planted seeds and picked weeds outside on the farm; others chopped vegetables in the kitchen or did laundry.

Of course, they also did things that most kids do today, such as studying, reading, and playing games. They worked hard, but they had fun too. Most black people in Mississippi were poor back then, and many had never been given the chance to learn how to read or write. Piney Woods was a hope-filled place.

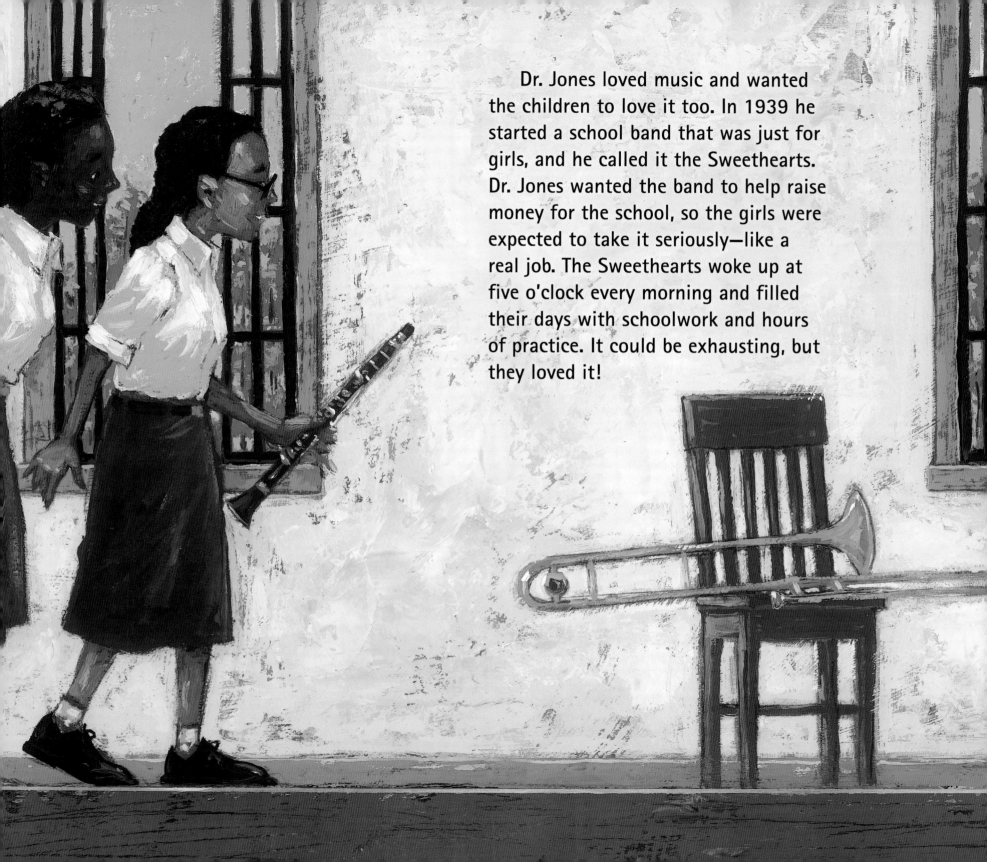

Dr. Jones loved music and wanted the children to love it too. In 1939 he started a school band that was just for girls, and he called it the Sweethearts. Dr. Jones wanted the band to help raise money for the school, so the girls were expected to take it seriously—like a real job. The Sweethearts woke up at five o'clock every morning and filled their days with schoolwork and hours of practice. It could be exhausting, but they loved it!

The music the girls played was called swing. Sometimes people called it big band music, because there were lots of instruments and musicians—sometimes as many as seventeen. The musicians were divided into sections, depending on what kind of instruments they played. The brass section was made up of trumpets and trombones. The woodwind

section had clarinets and saxophones. The rhythm section was all about drums, piano, bass, and guitars. There was one singer who was the leader, like a conductor, who kept the girls together at the right tempo. And the Sweethearts had a music coach who taught them new songs and put their music together for them.

SWING—now, that music was filled with energy! It was JAZZ. It had rhythms and melodies that got people up on their feet to dance. And like any good music, it told stories about how it feels to be alive. The Sweethearts played in churches and schools and other places.

When the girls left Piney Woods, they kept the Sweethearts together and moved to Washington DC, where they hoped to make a living as musicians.

They lived like a family of sisters, spending all their time together—eating, sleeping, talking, and playing music. Occasionally they got into fights, like sisters sometimes do. But mostly they got along.

They had a chaperone named Rae Lee Jones to look after them.

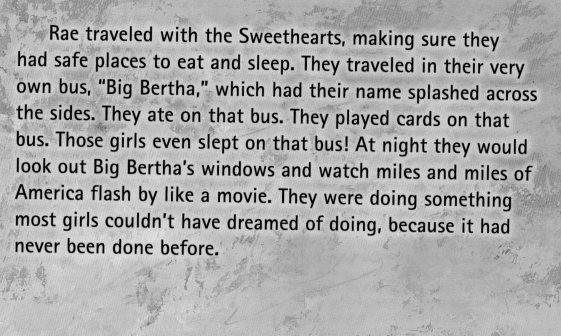

Rae traveled with the Sweethearts, making sure they had safe places to eat and sleep. They traveled in their very own bus, "Big Bertha," which had their name splashed across the sides. They ate on that bus. They played cards on that bus. Those girls even slept on that bus! At night they would look out Big Bertha's windows and watch miles and miles of America flash by like a movie. They were doing something most girls couldn't have dreamed of doing, because it had never been done before.

Every so often a band member would leave, but they were always picking up new musicians along the way: a sax player from Boston, a bass player from New York. The original members of the group were black, but the band grew to include people of many races and nationalities. The Sweethearts didn't care as long as they could play music. As long as they could *swing*.

They started calling themselves the International Sweethearts of Rhythm, and pretty soon they found themselves in the big-time. They got dressed up in beautiful gowns and fancy shoes, and performed for crowds all over the place. One week they played the Howard Theater in Washington, and thirty-five thousand people came to see them. The International Sweethearts were a sensation! People lined up in the streets for hours to hear them play.

Inside the theater, people danced in the aisles night after night.

In the 1940s there were other big band entertainers who were very popular, such as Louis Armstrong and Count Basie. They were leaders of male bands. The International Sweethearts of Rhythm was one of the very few all-female bands at the time. Women were discriminated against. They didn't get paid as much as male entertainers. Some people didn't take them seriously, but the Sweethearts worked just as hard as men did. And these women were good!

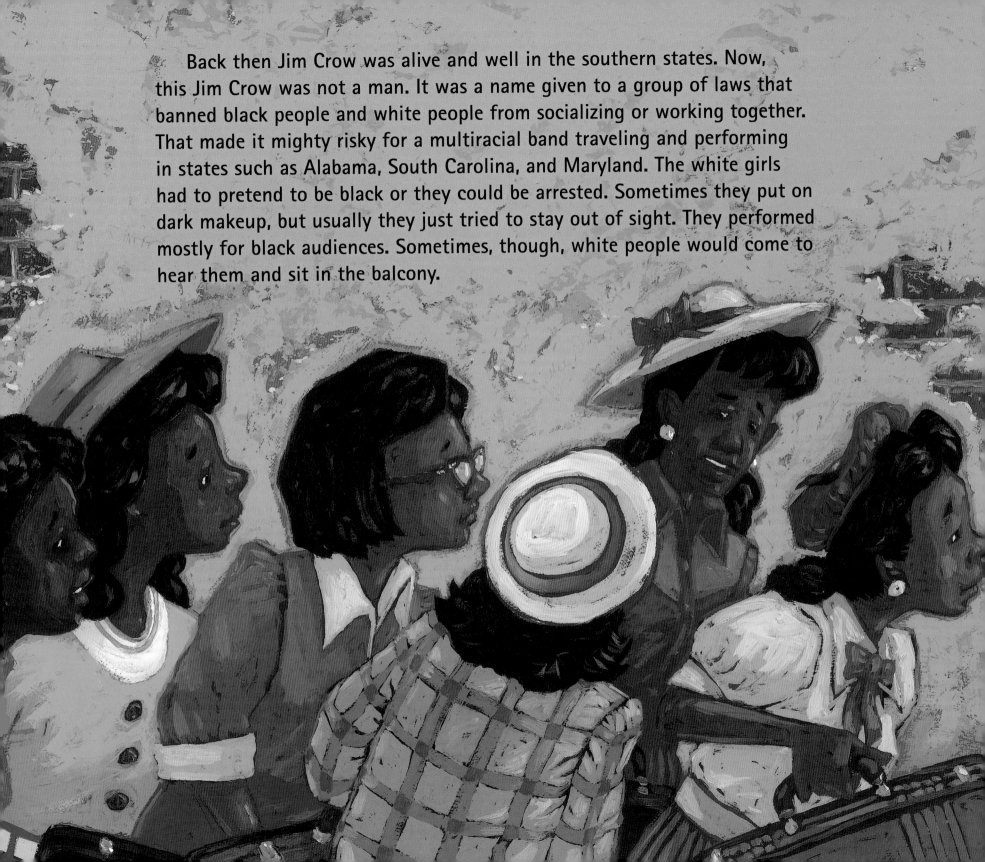

Back then Jim Crow was alive and well in the southern states. Now, this Jim Crow was not a man. It was a name given to a group of laws that banned black people and white people from socializing or working together. That made it mighty risky for a multiracial band traveling and performing in states such as Alabama, South Carolina, and Maryland. The white girls had to pretend to be black or they could be arrested. Sometimes they put on dark makeup, but usually they just tried to stay out of sight. They performed mostly for black audiences. Sometimes, though, white people would come to hear them and sit in the balcony.

Once while the Sweethearts were playing in a southern town, some policemen heard there were young white women in the band. The policemen started searching the bus, but the women escaped. They jumped into a taxi and headed straight for the train station. The taxi driver was scared because he didn't want to get in trouble. He was sure glad to say good-bye to them!

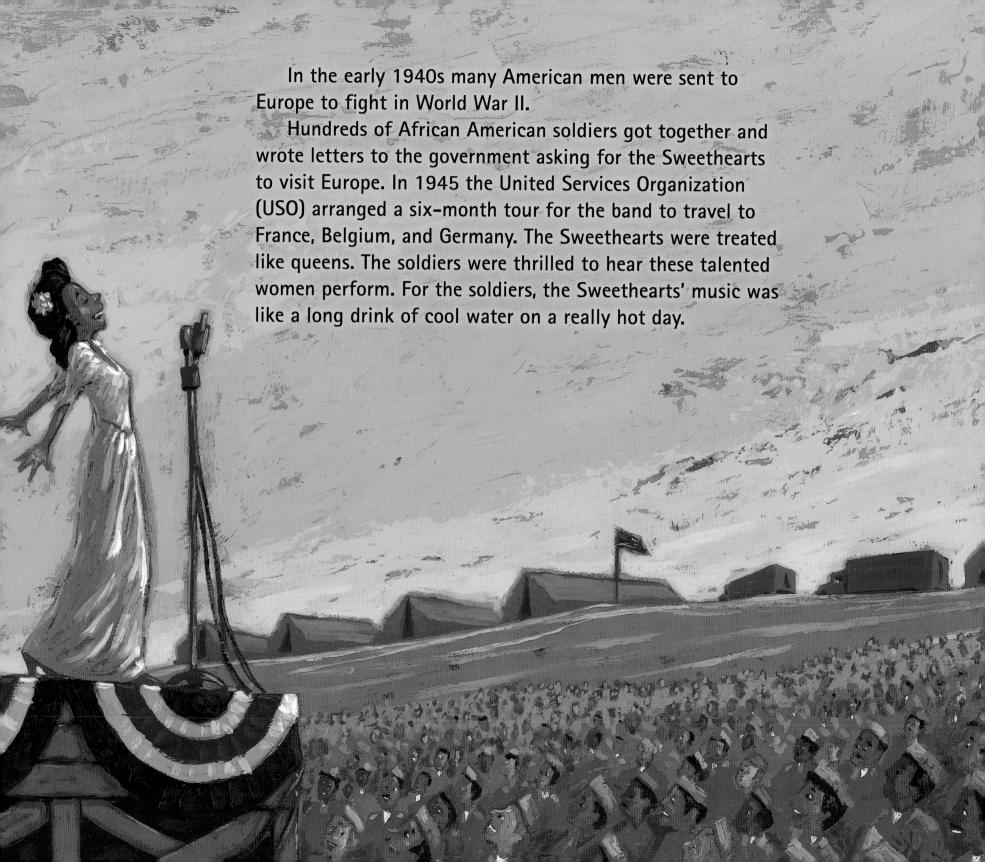

In the early 1940s many American men were sent to Europe to fight in World War II.

Hundreds of African American soldiers got together and wrote letters to the government asking for the Sweethearts to visit Europe. In 1945 the United Services Organization (USO) arranged a six-month tour for the band to travel to France, Belgium, and Germany. The Sweethearts were treated like queens. The soldiers were thrilled to hear these talented women perform. For the soldiers, the Sweethearts' music was like a long drink of cool water on a really hot day.

The Sweethearts came home and played for a while. They didn't make all that much money, though, and before long they started to go their separate ways.

Some got married and raised families. Some got other jobs. Some kept playing music for the rest of their lives.

In a way, though, they all made a difference. Those Sweethearts didn't know it at the time, but they helped open doors for women of all backgrounds. They gave hope to those who heard them play. And they helped show the world how to *swing*!

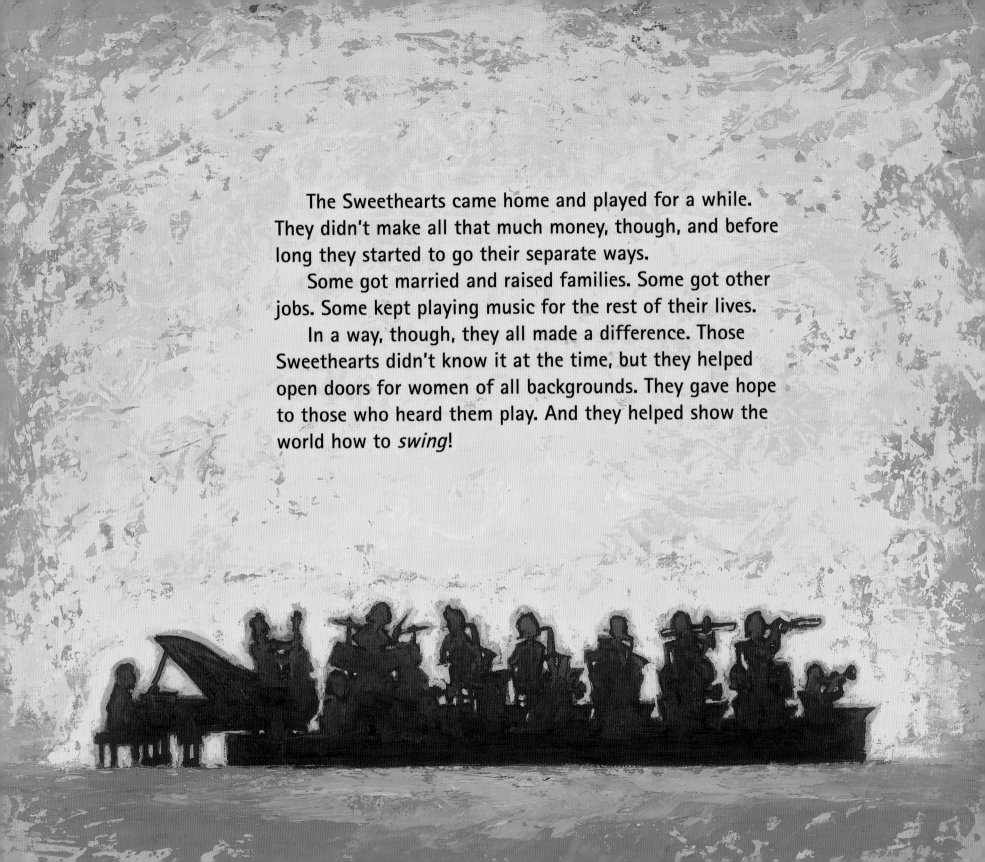

Author's Note

In spring 2011, five members of the International Sweethearts of Rhythm gathered onstage at the Smithsonian Institution for a conversation about women in jazz and the legacy of their band. They shared memories of joy and struggle during their trailblazing years on the jazz circuit. They also spoke of their commitment to getting an education, even as they pursued their musical aspirations. It's clear that, while these women were working hard and unknowingly making history, they were also having fun and building lasting friendships. These lives well lived are an inspiration to women and men, young and old.

Selected Bibliography

Books

Handy, D. Antoinette. *The International Sweethearts of Rhythm: The Ladies Jazz Band from Piney Woods Country Life School.* Lanham, MD, and London: The Scarecrow Press, Inc., 1998.

Nelson, Marilyn. *Sweethearts of Rhythm.* New York: Dial Books, 2009.

Placksin, Sally. *American Women in Jazz: 1900 to the Present.* (Publisher's city unavailable): Wideview Books, 1982.

Documentaries

The Girls in the Band. Directed by Judy Chaikin. Studio City, CA: One Step Productions, 2013.

The International Sweethearts of Rhythm. Directed by Greta Schiller and Andrea Weiss. New York: Jezebel Productions, 1986.

Websites

Campagna, Jeff. "Those Sweethearts Got Rhythm." *Smithsonian.com,* April 6, 2011. http://www.smithsonianmag.com/smithsonian-institution/those-sweethearts-got-rhythm-177264796/.

McDonough, John. "America's 'Sweethearts': An All-Girl Band That Broke Racial Boundaries." *NPR Music,* March 22, 2011. http://www.npr.org/2011/03/22/134766828/americas-sweethearts-an-all-girl-band-that-broke-racial-boundaries.